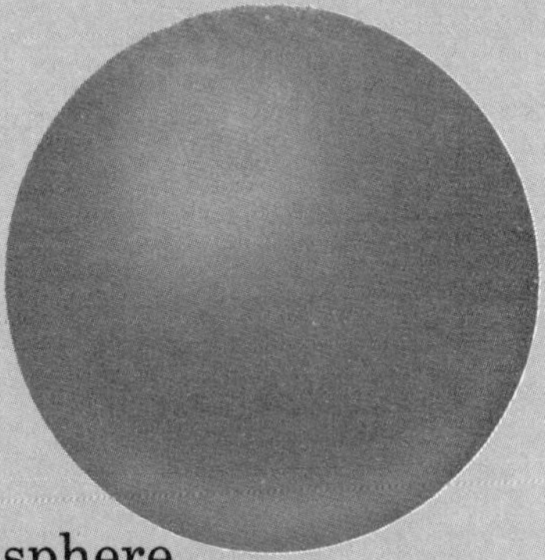
sphere

cone

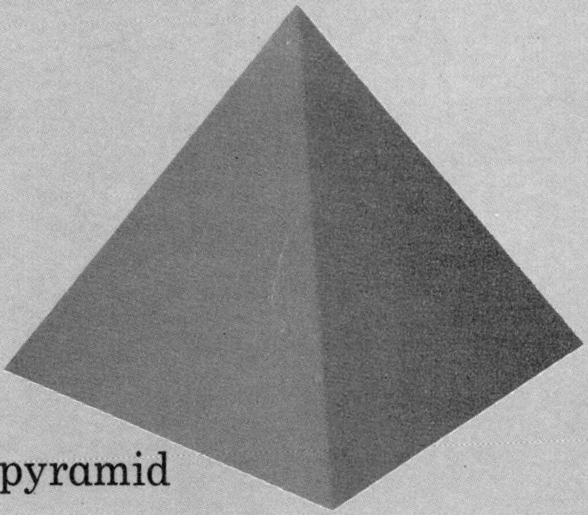
pyramid

cube

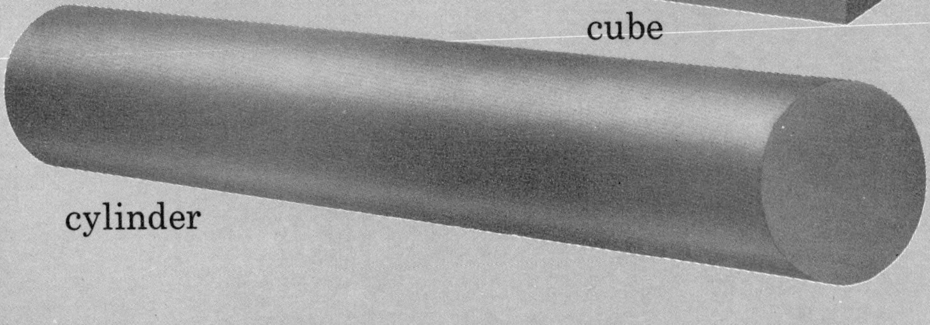
cylinder

First Published in 1970 by
Macdonald and Company
(Publishers) Limited
London W1
England

Managing Editor
Michael W. Dempsey B.A.

Chief Editor
Angela Sheehan B.A.

ISBN 0-7700-0335-4

Printed and bound in Great Britain

RYERSON FIRST LIBRARY

Number

THE RYERSON PRESS
Toronto Winnipeg Vancouver

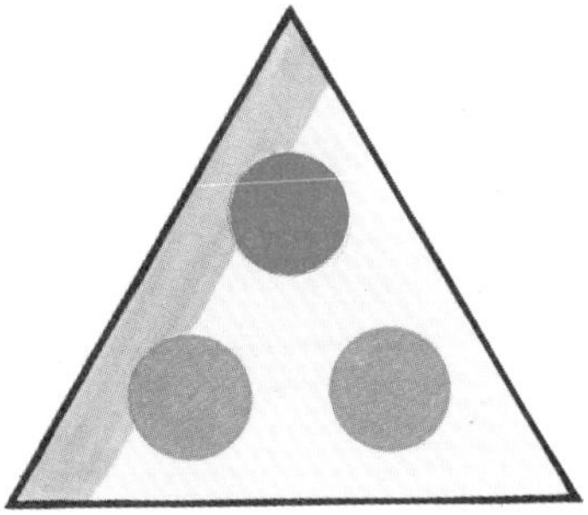

These are magic squares.

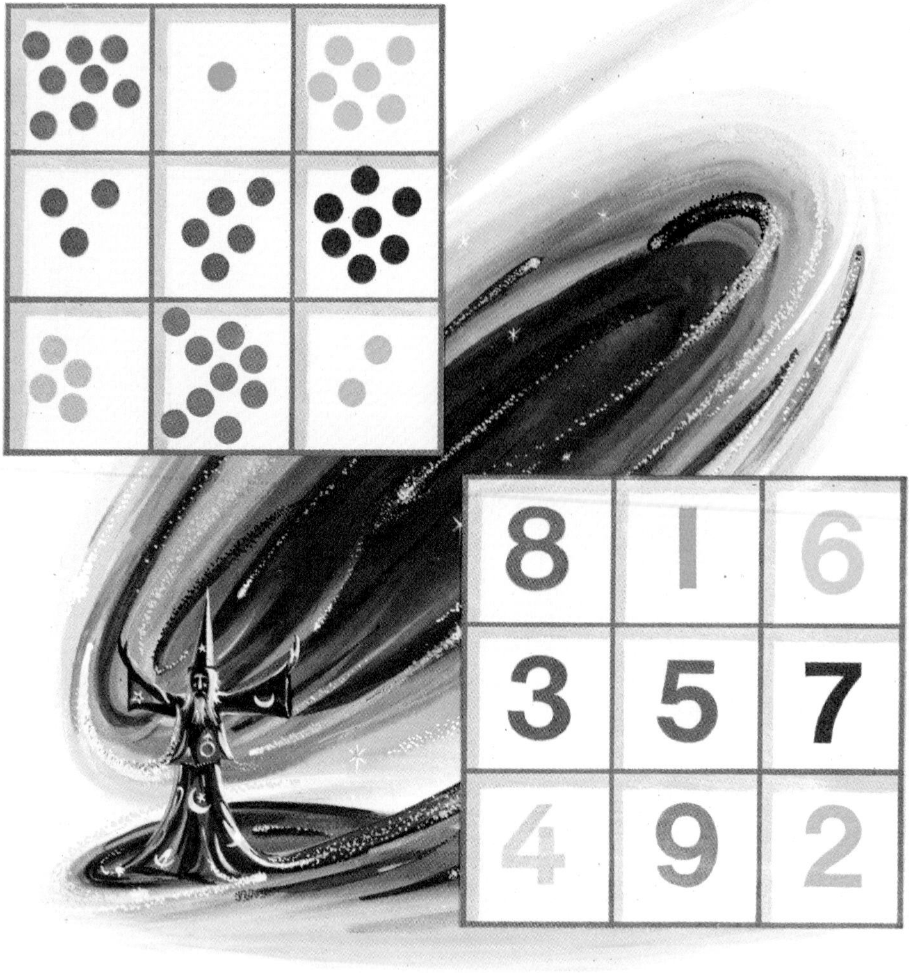

They are magic because
every row adds up
to the same number.

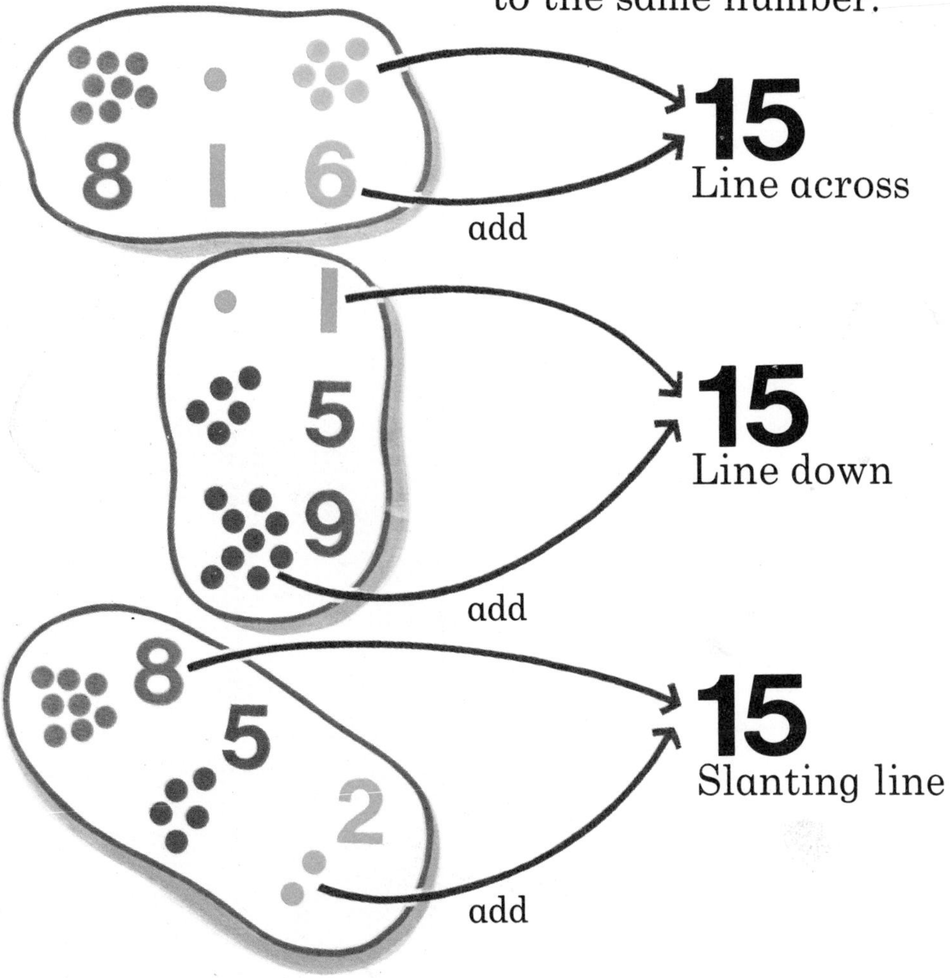

Here are some more magic squares.

4	9	2
3	5	7
8	1	6

6	1	8
7	5	3
2	9	4

2	7	6
9	5	1
4	3	8

6	7	2
1	5	9
8	3	4

In the first magic square the number signs
1, 2, 3, 4, 5, 6, 7, 8, 9 were used.
These signs are used, with the 0 sign, for
numbers in most parts of the world today.
But it was not always so.
The Romans used these signs.

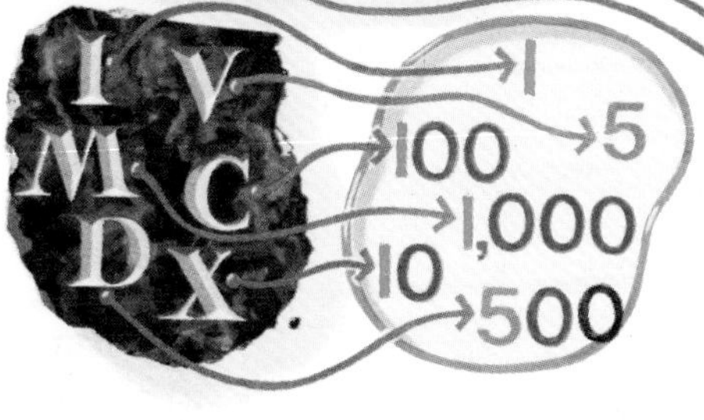

The Romans had no
sign for zero (0).

Cavemen did not have words or number signs to show how many hunters and animals there were. They painted them on the wall.

Long ago the Maya people, who lived in Mexico, used their fingers and toes to count.

They carved pictures of their number signs on blocks of stone.

Xul (5)

Muan (10)

The Incas of Peru tied knots in string.
They called them quipus.
They used them for counting the harvest.
One knot stood for each sheaf of wheat.

Some men cut notches in trees and sticks to count the days, weeks, and months of the year.
One notch stood for a day.

They called the sticks tally sticks.

Many people used an abacus for counting.

This man is an Assyrian. He has made an abacus in the sand to help him count.

This Roman is counting his soldiers.

Hindu abacus

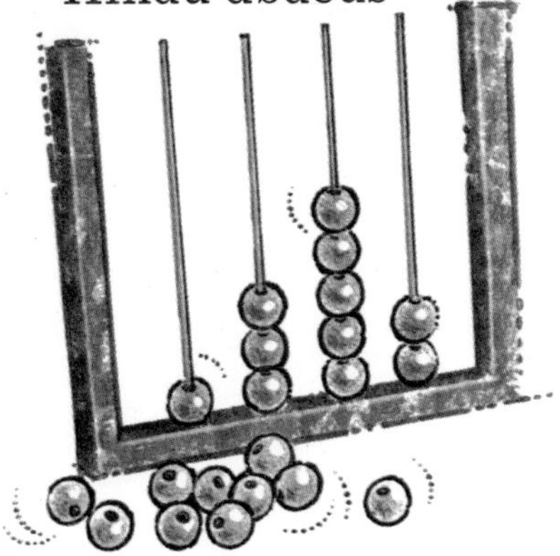

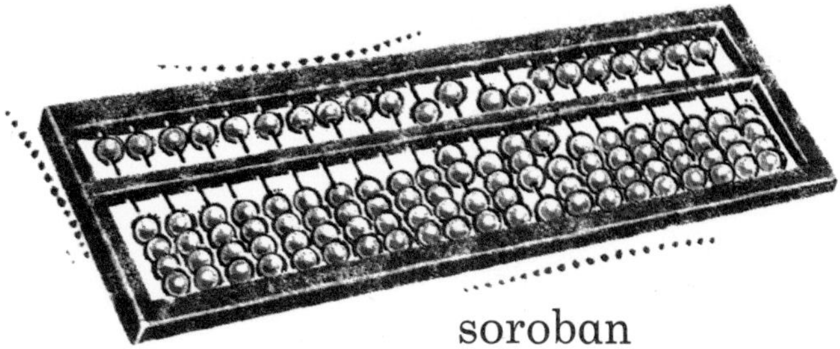

soroban

The Hindus used an abacus a long time ago.
The Japanese still use an abacus.
We call it a soroban.

Today we can use machines to help us count.

Numbers in nature

one

two

three

four

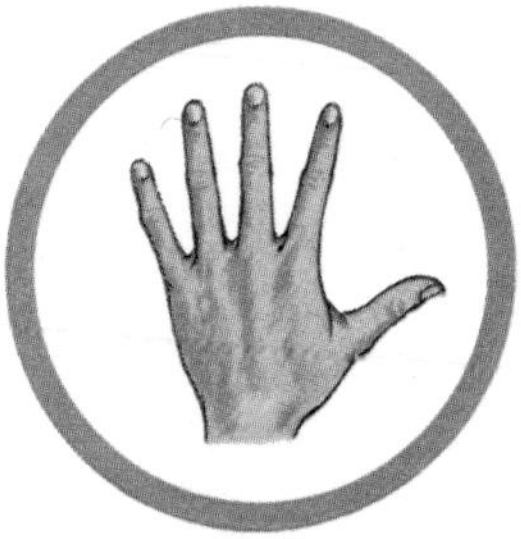

five

six

seven

eight

nine

Ones

‘Solo’ means one.
A soloist plays on his own.

‘Mono’ means one.
A monorail is a railway with only one rail.

‘Uni’ and ‘single’ are two more words which mean one.

Twos

'Bi' means two.
A bicycle has two wheels.

'Pair' means two.
There are two gloves in a pair.

'Duet' means two.
There are two people playing the piano.

'Dual' and 'twin' also mean two.

Rectangular numbers

We can arrange all numbers into rectangles but only some numbers can be put into rectangles of two rows.
These are rectangular numbers, or even numbers.

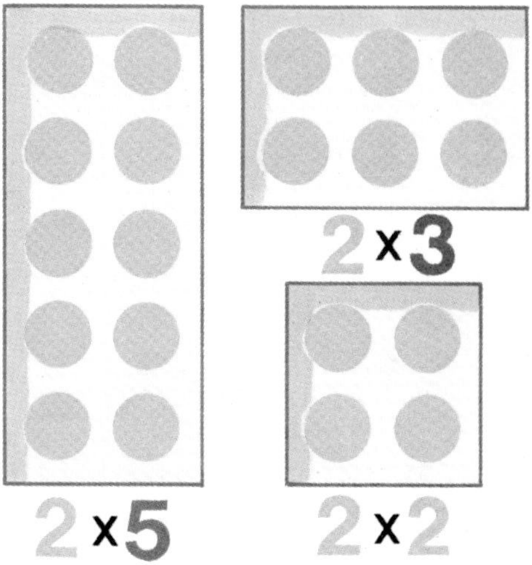

This is the pattern of two.
We counted in twos and coloured the squares we landed on.

1	2	3	4	5	6	7	8	9	10
11	12	13	14	15	16	17	18	19	20
21	22	23	24	25	26	27	28	29	30
31	32	33	34	35	36	37	38	39	40
41	42	43	44	45	46	47	48	49	50
51	52	53	54	55	56	57	58	59	60
61	62	63	64	65	66	67	68	69	70
71	72	73	74	75	76	77	78	79	80
81	82	83	84	85	86	87	88	89	90
91	92	93	94	95	96	97	98	99	100

Threes

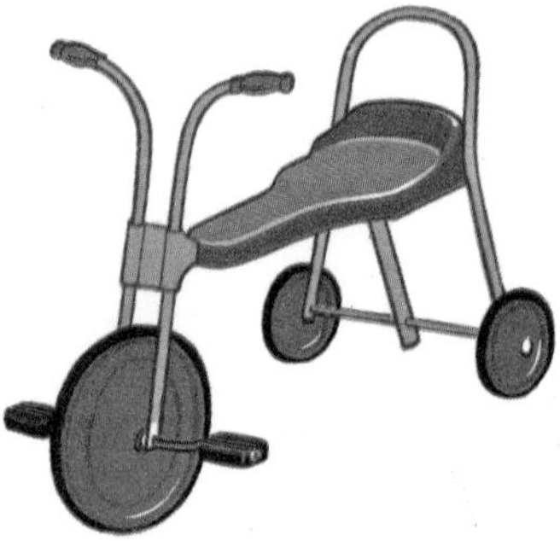

'Tri' means three.
A tricycle has three wheels.

King Neptune's trident had three prongs.

Triangular numbers

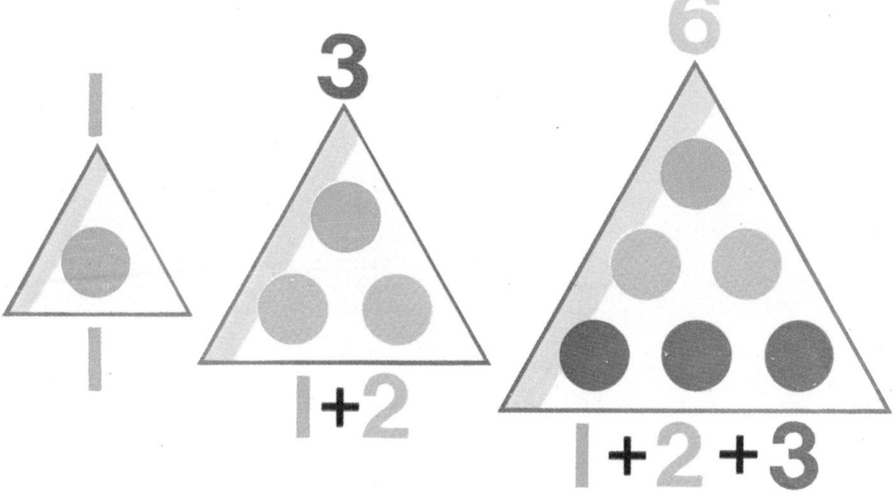

Each row has one more bead than the row above.

This is the pattern
of three.
We counted in threes
and coloured the
squares we landed on.

1	2	3	4	5	6	7	8	9	10
11	12	13	14	15	16	17	18	19	20
21	22	23	24	25	26	27	28	29	30
31	32	33	34	35	36	37	38	39	40
41	42	43	44	45	46	47	48	49	50
51	52	53	54	55	56	57	58	59	60
61	62	63	64	65	66	67	68	69	70
71	72	73	74	75	76	77	78	79	80
81	82	83	84	85	86	87	88	89	90
91	92	93	94	95	96	97	98	99	100

0 → 4 → 8 → 12 → 16 → 20 → 24 → 28 → 32

Fours

'Quad' means four.

Animals with four legs are quadrupeds.

These shapes are all quadrilaterals.

Square numbers

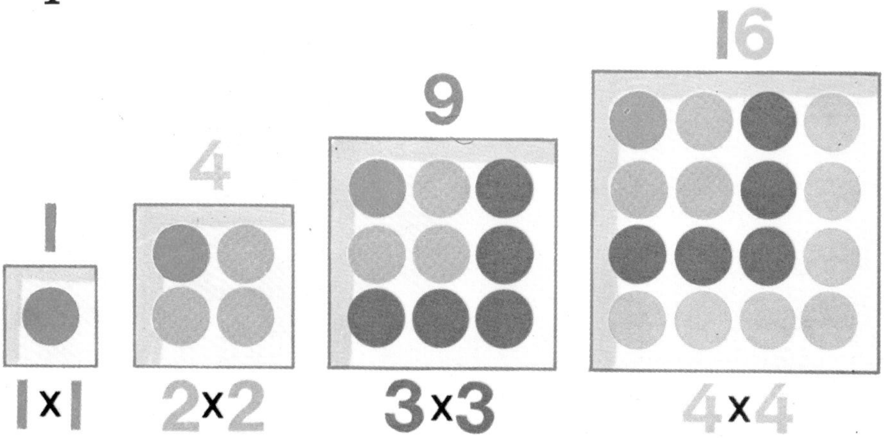

Each row and each column must have the same number of beads.

This is the pattern of four.
We counted in fours and coloured the squares we landed on.

1	2	3	**4**	5	6	7	**8**	9	10
11	**12**	13	14	15	**16**	17	18	19	**20**
21	22	23	**24**	25	26	27	**28**	29	30
31	**32**	33	34	35	**36**	37	38	39	**40**
41	42	43	**44**	45	46	47	**48**	49	50
51	**52**	53	54	55	**56**	57	58	59	**60**
61	62	63	**64**	65	66	67	**68**	69	70
71	**72**	73	74	75	**76**	77	78	79	**80**
81	82	83	**84**	85	86	87	**88**	89	90
91	**92**	93	94	95	**96**	97	98	99	**100**

Fives

'Quin' and 'pent' mean five.

There are five players in a quintet.

Pentominoes are shapes made from five squares. There are twelve different pentominoes.

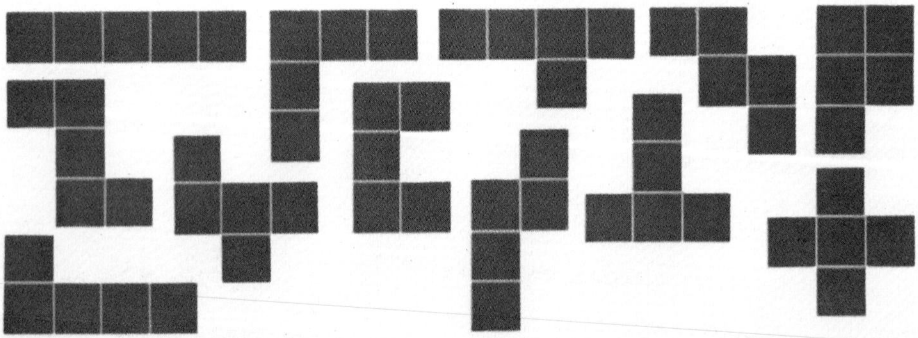

The pentomino puzzle

You can fit pentominoes together to make rectangles.

Using 4 pieces

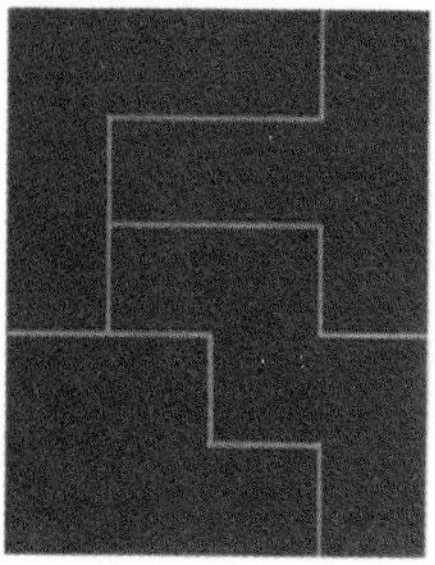

Using 12 pieces

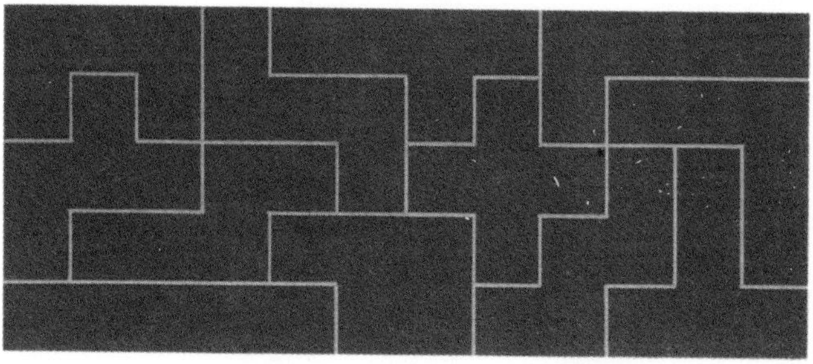

This is the pattern of five.
We counted in fives and coloured the squares we landed on.

1	2	3	4	5	6	7	8	9	10
11	12	13	14	15	16	17	18	19	20
21	22	23	24	25	26	27	28	29	30
31	32	33	34	35	36	37	38	39	40
41	42	43	44	45	46	47	48	49	50
51	52	53	54	55	56	57	58	59	60
61	62	63	64	65	66	67	68	69	70
71	72	73	74	75	76	77	78	79	80
81	82	83	84	85	86	87	88	89	90
91	92	93	94	95	96	97	98	99	100

Sixes

'Hex' means six.

Insects are hexapods.
They have six legs.

This shape is the hexagram. It has six points.

1	2	3	4	5	6	7	8	9	10
11	12	13	14	15	16	17	18	19	20
21	22	23	24	25	26	27	28	29	30
31	32	33	34	35	36	37	38	39	40
41	42	43	44	45	46	47	48	49	50
51	52	53	54	55	56	57	58	59	60
61	62	63	64	65	66	67	68	69	70
71	72	73	74	75	76	77	78	79	80
81	82	83	84	85	86	87	88	89	90
91	92	93	94	95	96	97	98	99	100

This is the pattern of six.
We counted in sixes and coloured the squares we landed on.

→7→14→21→28→35→42→49→56

Sevens

'Hept' means seven.

The heptagon has seven sides.

There are seven days in the week. There are seven colours in the rainbow. They are violet, indigo, blue, green, yellow, orange and red.

This is the pattern of seven. We counted in sevens and coloured the squares we landed on.

1	2	3	4	5	6	7	8	9	10
11	12	13	14	15	16	17	18	19	20
21	22	23	24	25	26	27	28	29	30
31	32	33	34	35	36	37	38	39	40
41	42	43	44	45	46	47	48	49	50
51	52	53	54	55	56	57	58	59	60
61	62	63	64	65	66	67	68	69	70
71	72	73	74	75	76	77	78	79	80
81	82	83	84	85	86	87	88	89	90
91	92	93	94	95	96	97	98	99	100

0 → 8 → 16 → 24 → 32 → 40 → 48 → 56

Eights

'Oct' means eight.
An octopus has eight tentacles.

1	2	3	4	5	6	7	8	9	10
11	12	13	14	15	16	17	18	19	20
21	22	23	24	25	26	27	28	29	30
31	32	33	34	35	36	37	38	39	40
41	42	43	44	45	46	47	48	49	50
51	52	53	54	55	56	57	58	59	60
61	62	63	64	65	66	67	68	69	70
71	72	73	74	75	76	77	78	79	80
81	82	83	84	85	86	87	88	89	90
91	92	93	94	95	96	97	98	99	100

This is the pattern of eight.
We counted in eights and coloured the squares we landed on.

0 → 9 → 18 → 27 → 36 → 45 → 54 → 63 → 72

Nines

9 This is the number sign for the biggest amount that we can have in the units, tens, hundreds, thousands and so on.

The abacus says 9. Add 1 and it looks like this.

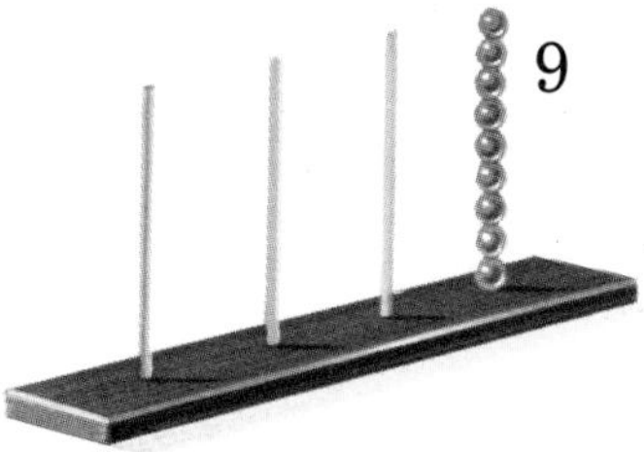

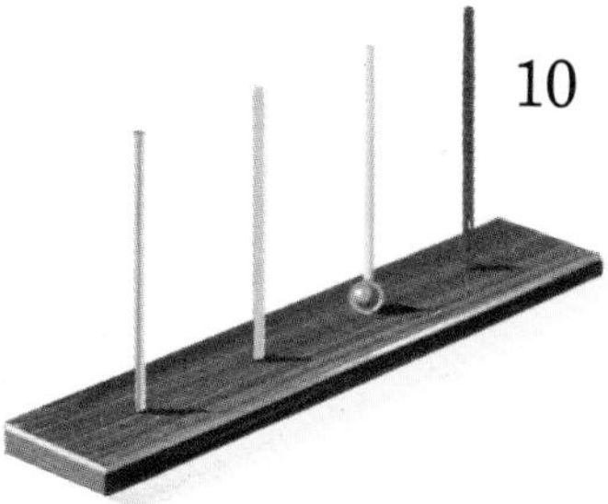

This is the pattern of nine.
We counted in nines and coloured the squares we landed on.

1	2	3	4	5	6	7	8	9	10
11	12	13	14	15	16	17	18	19	20
21	22	23	24	25	26	27	28	29	30
31	32	33	34	35	36	37	38	39	40
41	42	43	44	45	46	47	48	49	50
51	52	53	54	55	56	57	58	59	60
61	62	63	64	65	66	67	68	69	70
71	72	73	74	75	76	77	78	79	80
81	82	83	84	85	86	87	88	89	90
91	92	93	94	95	96	97	98	99	100

Prime numbers

Some numbers can be arranged in rectangles of more than one row, like this:

6 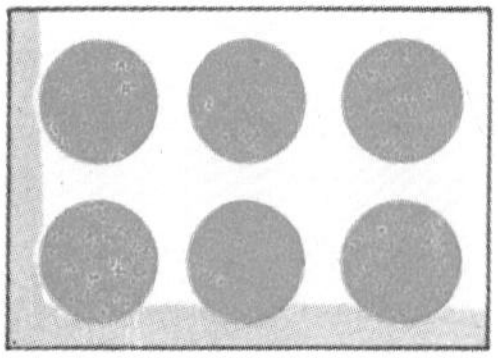 or 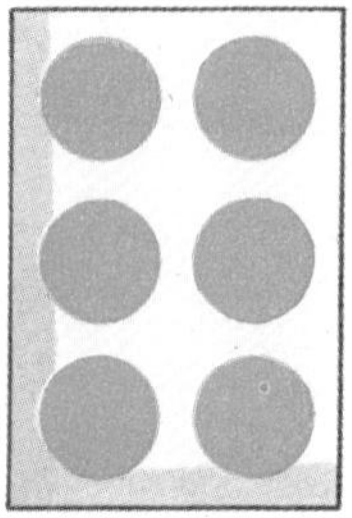

Some numbers can only be arranged in a rectangle which has just one row, like this:

2
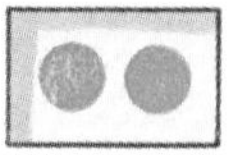
3
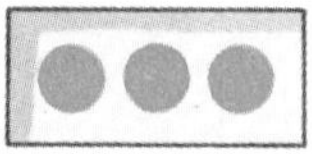
5
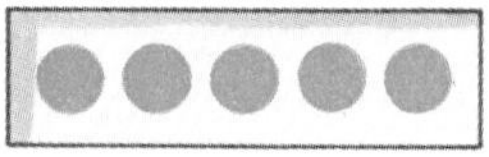
7
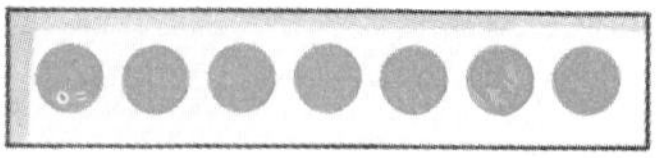
11
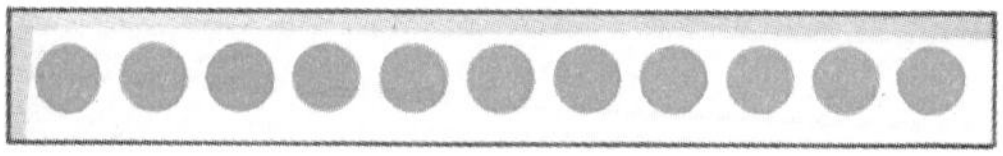

and so on

Numbers which can only be arranged in a single row are called prime numbers.

1	2	3	4	5	6	7	8	9	10
11	12	13	14	15	16	17	18	19	20
21	22	23	24	25	26	27	28	29	30
31	32	33	34	35	36	37	38	39	40
41	42	43	44	45	46	47	48	49	50
51	52	53	54	55	56	57	58	59	60
61	62	63	64	65	66	67	68	69	70
71	72	73	74	75	76	77	78	79	80
81	82	83	84	85	86	87	88	89	90
91	92	93	94	95	96	97	98	99	100

In this square all the number patterns have been put on top of each other in one square. Notice that 2, 3, 5, 7 and the other numbers which are not coloured are prime numbers.

Place value

Here is a big number in number signs. 1000

1000 is much bigger than 1. Look!

one thousand

one unit

On the abacus one unit looks like this.

1000 looks like this.

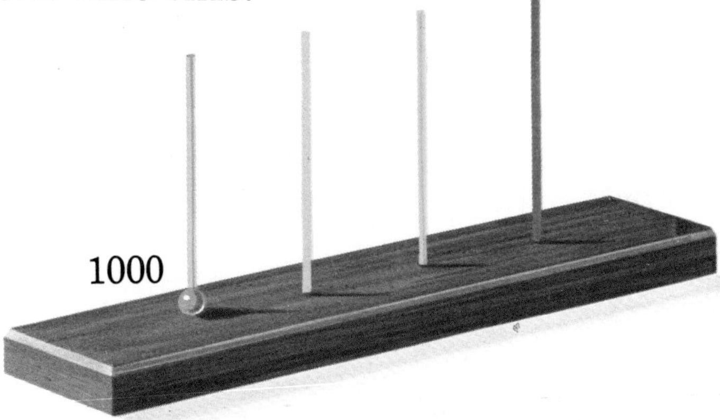

There is still only one bead on the abacus but it is not in the same place.

Here are two more numbers. 100 and 10

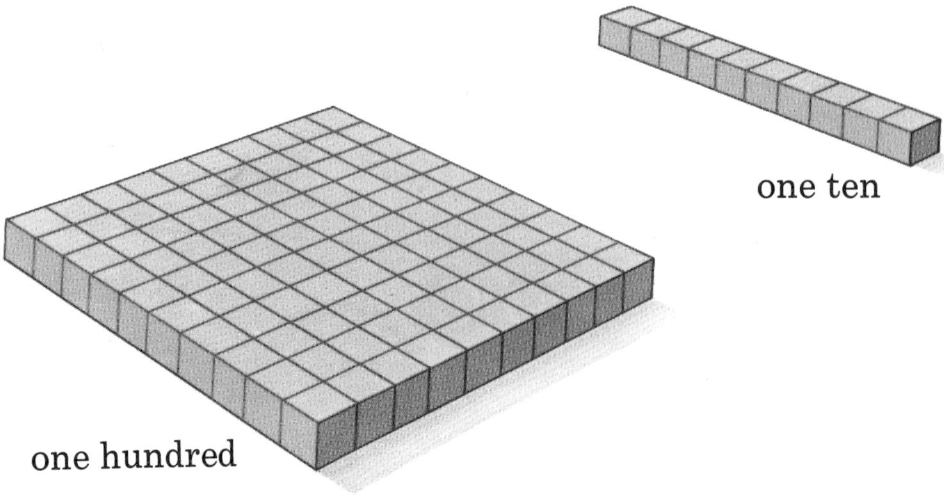

On the abacus they look like this.

All these numbers can be shown by just one bead on the abacus but the bead must be in the right place.

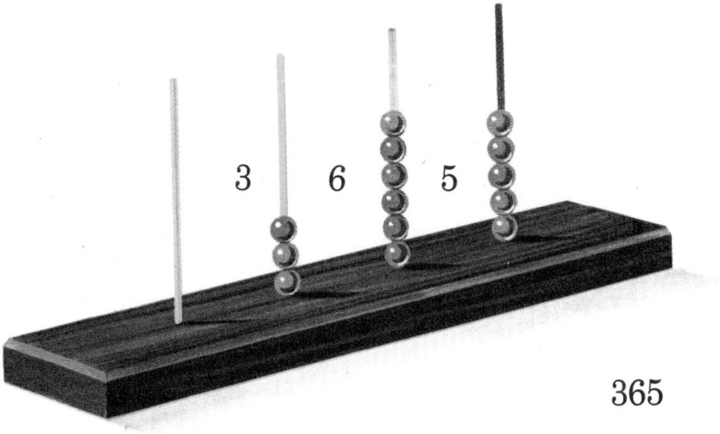

365—three hundred and sixty five—is shown on the abacus. Five beads on the units rod means 5. Six beads on the tens rod means 60. Three beads on the hundreds rod means 300. Altogether it means 365—the number of days in one year.

Index

triangle

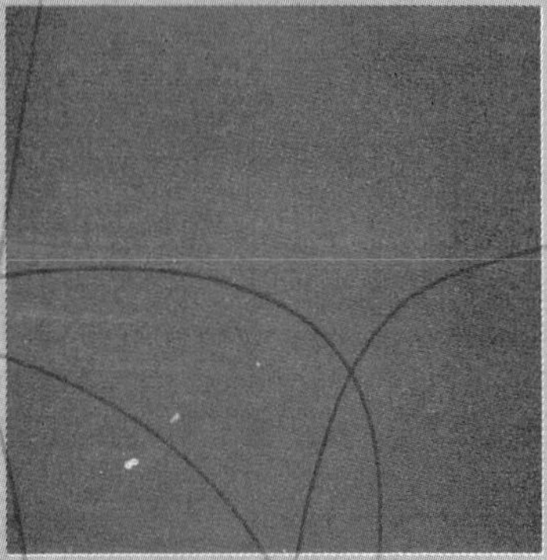

square

pentagon

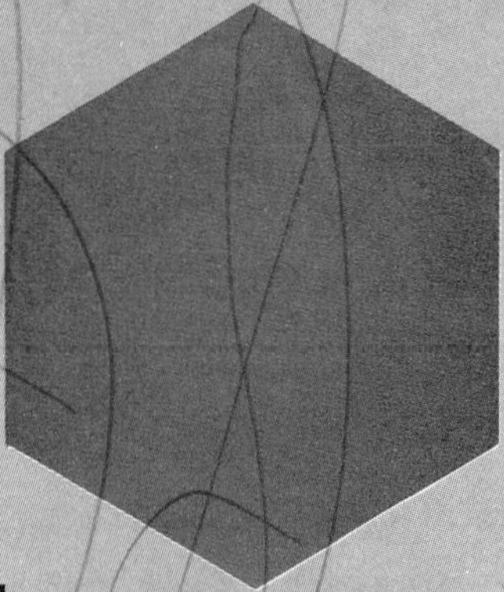

hexagon

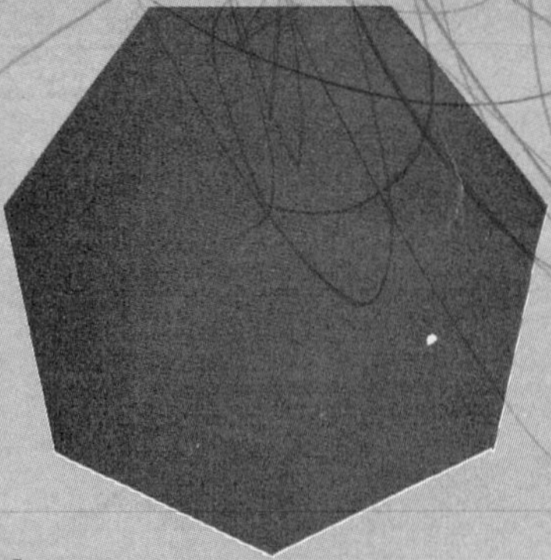

heptagon

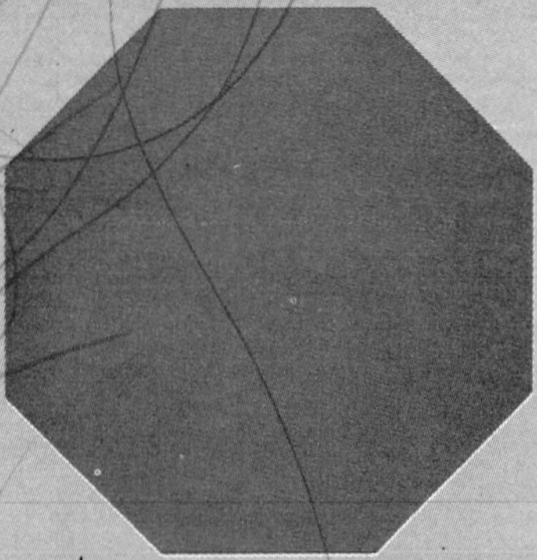

octagon